# The Unrequited

# THE UNREQUITED

POEMS

## Carrie St. George Comer

Winner of the 2002
Kathryn A. Morton Prize in Poetry
Selected by Stephen Dunn

Sarabande  Books

LOUISVILLE, KENTUCKY

No part of this book may be reproduced without written permission of the publisher. Please direct inquiries to:

> Managing Editor
> Sarabande Books, Inc.
> 2234 Dundee Road, Suite 200
> Louisville, KY 40205

Library of Congress Cataloging-in-Publication Data

Comer, Carrie St. George, 1971-
  The unrequited : poems / by Carrie St. George Comer.— 1st ed.
   p. cm.
  "Winner of the 2002 Kathryn A. Morton Prize in Poetry."
  ISBN 1-889330-94-9 (acid-free paper) — ISBN 1-889330-95-7 (pbk. : acid-free paper)
  I. Title.
PS3603.O58 U57 2003
811'.6—dc21              2002153429

Cover image: *Dawn, 1990,* by Odd Nerdrum. © Odd Nerdrum, courtesy of Forum Gallery, New York

Cover and text design by Charles Casey Martin

Manufactured in the United States of America.
This book is printed on acid-free paper.

Sarabande Books is a nonprofit literary organization.

---

Special thanks to the following most generous supporters: Anonymous (2), Anne Axton, Kurt Brown, Steffanie Brown, Dick and Jeanne Fisher, The Murray and Grace Gissman Foundation, Charles and Roberta Graham, Nancy and Dick Graham, Lisa Brown and Daniel Handler, Susan Griffin and Douglas Sharps, James Baker Hall, John Jacob, Nancy Lampton, Al Lyons, Peter Saunders, The Sunrise Fund, James and Marianne Welch, Jean West, and the Robert Winthrop Charitable Trust.

FIRST EDITION

Who is shaking us? Who?

—Yehuda Amichai

# CONTENTS

# ACKNOWLEDGMENTS

*The American Poetry Review:* "Tongues," "The Primitive Model"

*Web Conjunctions:* "Shelburne Falls"

*New Orleans Review:* "The Iris of the Pig"

*The Black Warrior Review:* "Local Art"

*Pleiades:* "Vespers"

*Fence:* "Even Donkeys"

*Conduit:* "Noiseless and Small"

*The Hollins Critic:* "The Difference Between This Moment and the
Next"

*ONTHEBUS:* "Get Outta Town"

*The Laurel Review:* "Weakness #1: The Barber," "Weakness #2:
The Barber"

*Denver Quarterly:* "Wine"

*Washington Square:* "Circles"

*NC1:* "La Reforma"


"Local Art" received *The Black Warrior Review* Poetry Prize, selected
by Joel Brouwer.

# INTRODUCTION

On the day I read Carrie St. George Comer's *The Unrequited* for the third time, I had just finished a wonderful essay by Donald Barthelme called "Not-Knowing." It was about the mysteries of composition and contained within it a story that was wryly illustrative of its points, which enabled him to earn his more philosophical language. So there's a great deal of fun and invention intermixed with sentences that talk about "...the combinatorial agility of words, the exponential generation of meaning once they've been allowed to go to bed together." And the simpler but no less incisive, "Art is a true account of the activity of the mind."

Barthelme had prepared me, in the curious way that such things happen, to properly receive and appreciate the distinctive verbal dash of Comer's manuscript, and the quicksilver mind behind it. Page after page, the recognizably-real and the imaginative flirt with and complement one another, while the tonalities we hear and feel seem to be informed by a rare blend of play and lament. And often the poems will have this kind of enigmatic clarity:

The outer life rings distantly,

a tiny spoon tapping a tiny boat.

Or this kind:

...This is not killing me, it's not. That's not your car
parked outside the house, and that wasn't you I saw

waving from a windy field. That was a blue-gray rag tied
to a stick.

I've always believed that our feelings need as much intelligence as we can give them, just as our intellect needs to find its passions. A good mind simultaneously registers and embodies. Comer's rhythms authenticate what she asserts. Even when moments in her poems elude me, the authority of her voice keeps me in and with their drift. Or, as in some of the longer poems, images and claims, some of them strange, accumulate associatively and impressionistically. They leave us with a true account of the activity of a mind.

— *Stephen Dunn*

The Unrequited

# The Difference Between This Moment
# and the Next

Drinking steadily in a grand hotel, my thoughts were simple:

a glass of red wine is a garnet,
the palm of a hand the inner chamber of a shell,
the fingernails painted deep as garnets.

A net of white flowers
broke over the buildings and I was mapping out

my life again, drawing figures on a paper napkin
of how it should look and where it will end. When the city's gone,
the shadows remain: shadows jogging down tree-lined streets,

shadows eating blue ice cream,
shadows driving around in long black cars, at the center of each
a nucleus of light like the forehead of a slow-moving horse.

Yesterday in a glass house, a blue morpho landed on my coat,

his irides throbbing like plums, his wings closing and turning umber,
his slow proboscis touching me; patient as a gondola,

he blew into my life and out again.

And what of the dismal boy I coaxed into my room before the storm.
I wanted him to die in my arms but he died alone, headed east
twelve hours later. It's surprising,

the way a memory will bury itself
and emerge again long after the body that left it here.

The desert waits six million years to reveal a footprint.

A strange eyelash touched down on my pillow, skilled as an insect wing
departed from the insect. A stream of breath keeps rising from
   my teacup,

tiny trees are growing on the windowsill.

# Under Your Hat

A low wind sings
in the dead corn.
A gray web spreads
over the fields. Rain.
Last time we met
you were damp with
anguish; a snail
had died in your hand.
Finally, everything
is unrequited.
Or must be made so.

# Vespers

On a shoulder of interstate north of here
a man wraps a small dead wolf in newspaper.
I think he sees a movement in the eye,
some kind of reflection, a cloud swelling with snow
or a three-quarter day moon, the man's own head
when he leans to see if the wolf is still breathing.
What does the man see in the eye of the wolf?
It isn't a soul, wolves don't have those.
But he lays the body in the trunk of the car,
taking his time, and returns to the road and drives
to some other place. I suppose the man owns
a few acres where the wolf may be properly laid to rest.
A stem of phlox to mark the place, a brief prayer,
then back to the house with his sons,
who keep quiet because they know how hard the day
has been on their father. In his room, the sound of wolves
in snares, not a howling sound, no, a labored breath
through the nose. He walks the corridor till the sun falls
in rectangles on the floor. Beyond the trees,
pale blue mountains. Clouds breaststroke across the field.
What did the man find there, in the still black eye?
And why did he bury the wolf so close?
And will a plum tree be standing there come spring?

# Get Outta Town

Sometimes it's best to let things die, especially houseplants
given by friends. My dog believes if you turn your heart away
from something it dies and from there you can simply watch it go.
I've packed the things you left in the corners of what used to be
a shared home, and plan to mail them next week. Your pants
keep rustling around in the box. Your little animal statues,
I hear them too. Everyone says *have fun now, ride the racehorse
and keep kicking till he dies on you,* but I am tired and folly
closed itself in the garage with a running car. I found the body
this morning on my way out for a jog. It's hard to love someone
and hard not to, I can't keep up with which or don't want to. Funny
how big the room seems at first, and finally, how the bigness gets
crowded out by my circus of flowering vines and the tall boy that cares
for them. I keep the blinds closed and the bedclothes rumpled
on the off chance that you've forgotten something and need to swing by
one last time. This is not killing me, it's not. That's not your car
parked outside the house, and that wasn't you I saw
waving from a windy field. That was a blue-gray rag tied to a stick.

# Arbor

Do you remember the love?
Do you remember the passion that took place there?

*No.*

Do you remember the white fence? The vine of white blossom?

*Not really.*

Do you recall the white mug that rested on the wrought-iron table or the white gloves that lifted the mug to the thin lips?

*No. I don't remember any of that. I wasn't there.*

Oh, you were there alright. You couldn't get enough of those long gloves, those polished shoes, those flowers like stars that came through the trellis slats like grapes. White grapes. And white hair like a veil of wind. Do you remember? We rocked each other in bed at night when noises covered the old room like a hailstorm, like a wind in the frozen branches. It was Easter. There were hats everywhere. Hats trimmed with shells and magnolias and birds made with real feathers. Lilies wrapped around hats like stars. Remember the girl with grasshoppers in her hair?

*No. What color were they?*

White. Remember our camel journey? Remember the runaway camel? Remember the rings in his nose? His ankle bracelets? The great chains of jasmine he wore to ride through town? Remember the great chains of jasmine? Remember the abuse we took from the coffee lady? The curtains hanging everywhere? The mirrored pants? Do you remember those sickly sweet balls of dough dipped in syrup? The little moon stuck to her white dress? Not crescent, fully waxed, and red, like a spot of blood. I felt sick over everything I had ever done. Remember that?

*Not sure.*

Remember the murdered pigs and the women who dismembered them?

*God, no.*

Remember the guesthouses that were really brothels? That man that kept stroking your hair? The girls with numbers pinned to their dresses? The monkeys that ruled the town? The rooms were like enormous showers with barred windows. Remember the funerals that kept us up at night?

*What funerals? And what moon?*

Remember the time we blew each other under the stars? You know. I blew your schmetterling. You blew my papillon. Remember?

*No.*

Yes you do, you rode into town for daffodils because I said we must sound like tree frogs bathing in the throat of a daffodil. And as I lay there waiting in the grass, someone was throwing banana peels out of the neighbor's attic window. And I slept in the lingering scent of banana and daffodil. White banana. White daffodil. White grapes hanging in the air like little babies filled with light. And you don't remember?

*No, I don't remember.*

Do you remember anything, anything at all?

*Nope.*

Nothing at all?

*No, nothing at all.*

Well I could never forget. Someone was crying in the juniper bushes because we'd decided to grow old together. And someone was turning the garage into a planetarium. A milk truck stopped at every doorstep and the clinking bottles chased an egret into the clouds. Remember? A red sun rose and burned everything.

# Local Art

A bull crosses the mead with his bell swinging.

Stars, like nerve ends, tip the branches.
Oh José, how I age beneath the creaking arm

and all it wants is you to pick its figs.
They hang like iron balls on hooks. Oh José,

see the bellies of the fruit bats dusted with pollen:
wingéd lemons, ha ha.

They pump the white flowers till dawn.

In the gallery designed to simulate joy,
we bought a paper lily with a finger for a pistil.

We slept on the pull-out sofa,
and my heart began to rest:

dream of a shoe descending to a lake bottom,
the foot inside.

Soon I'll travel to your birthplace
and write you from a morning grove:

all night a butcher walked the aisles
in her paisley coat and silver loafers  stop
a host of wild pigs invaded the city  stop

Dear José, *sorry* is a pigeon bone

Dear José, in the proper glove
a pigeon bone is a flute, or a tool used to slay wild pigs.

The lips are a rose's misty print.

Last night I drove down 91. Eohippus cantered
in my side view
like a pupil in the starry eye, ha ha.

We once thought him the first primate.

Oh José, I waved to him.
And he, sweet cob, waved back.

# Don't Let Me Forget You

Memory: the enemy. Its nude and worthless body

enters the evening as if on wings, smiling and waving a white feather,
first quiet, then tanked,

but still a rating of G: for mild peril, for some scary images,

for emotional brutality.
When it sleeps, its prick hangs against the bedward thigh,

the tip rising, then dropping,
then sticking,

a bit of spank to hold its place, the prick long as a sonnet

and as thick, with a turn near the end.
A woman with a beetle in her hair asks if it was awful.

*Was it awful?* It wasn't so awful. We watch it sleep, then we sleep.

By morning it's gone, its print left in the sand
just inches from the sharky waters

where a lemon-yellow boy glides past in a sailboat.

# Tongues

The river carries a harvest of petals to the pond
where families drive around in rented boats. From here

I am big enough to pluck them from their vessels and make

a chain. By second grade, we learn we hear ourselves

through bone, so we don't really know what we sound like.
It can take weeks to string it all together, like shells with holes

we turn into jewelry for daughters who don't know how.
A vine dangles from my window like a wasted dictator,

the blood rushing to his head. Sometimes late, I hear him sobbing.

I am not old enough to speak of such things.
A man enters the room, I uncross myself

but what can I know of him? A cloud forms, he tells me his dreams:

*last night you performed the most stunning strip tease.*
*Your breasts, jesus, the sway and lift of them, pink funnels,*

*the way they sat up in spite of you and begged. So I did it,*

*I touched them and they gave it all up, the love you've been*
*hiding from me, the way you run into the bushes every time*

*you see me. It's not fair, the way you talk to me as if I have*

*rocks in my pockets, the way you take off your hat when*
*I'm around and toss it on the counter like a book you don't intend*

*to read or a slice of melon that suddenly went sour in your mouth.*

*Grotesque, your hat. I simply don't like it. And your shoes,*
*did I ever tell you that you wear very ugly shoes?*

We lie. We spit. It's called communication.

Sometimes he creeps up from behind and taps me
on the shoulder with a bony (not bony like spooky bony but

the kind of bony dogs go after or so we tell ourselves) finger.

I lied.

I looked down at my dirty dress and turned still as the rotted tree.

Like when you've just lost someone,

everyone else is just a little meaner and even you yourself
feel you could take a date to a hanging.

We were trying on gravity boots and doing shots.

For half a second, I felt the ignition of the head,
what it would be to die like the match.

The large body at the party, I thought,
was there to save me: an event across my barren landscape,

it wanted to touch my face. Twirling like a daffodil,

I said yes three times and offered up my best tale:
*once a Javan fruit bat climbed the arm of a Dutch tourist,*

*his wings enveloping the freckled skin, his tiny black penis unfurling.*

Lying in the quilts and sweating he told me
the rabbits in Guangzhou markets

*are strung up by the feet. They don't perish till butchered.*
.He said *this is a beautiful country but when I walk beneath*

*the flowering trees or drive through a town that worships its missing,*
*I think of old folk homes, incinerators, public restrooms.*
*I can't stay.*

And I said I'd never sleep knowing they're out there
all night with their eyes wide open,

each word a polished bead impaled on a thread.

My head thick as a plum,
my thorax a sexual x-ray, I woke.

Nothing had changed.
Everyone I knew before was still talking.

One, *death is a mirror of the life lived before it.*
Two, *parataxis is a form of dinosaur.*
Three, *the seeds of the foxglove may be used as a cardiac stimulant.*
Four, *you are held together by holes.*

I wear the low voices like rosary,
I walk from my mother's house to the live oak that commemorates
the men killed there. According to locals, bees

hold revivals in the leaves come every first of June.
So in a clump of trumpet pitchers, I watch for white tents,

and slow hymns blown like milkweed across the field.
The outer life rings distantly,

a tiny spoon tapping a tiny boat.

# A Note from Olive Lane

It said the trees here almost sing
and when you sit down to a bowl of soup
they set a branch on your placemat
in lieu of a spoon. There were drawings
in the margins of women in black shrouds
saying "in my country, this" "in my country,
that." It arrived in a green envelope
with seven different stamps and a fat check
inside, for which I was grateful. It arrived
just after a phone call from my father
telling me to drink more water if I want
to get better. It was slipped under the door.
It said the sun is bright but won't
hurt you and the rain only enhances
the soothing light and the apricot skin
that blesses the children. I carried it
around with me all day. I carried it deep
inside my saddlebag and did not take it out
until I was home again. With a day's journey
the note changed. The women in the margins
were no longer women but giraffes crossing
a yellow savannah and shouting
"The honor of your presence is requested
in the Blue Lounge at six o'clock sharp!"
It said it's hot out here, so you'll need
a featherweight sunbonnet and several layers

of mosquito netting. Don't forget
a sturdy bucket for the snails, there's not
much in the way of food. The river's been dry
for weeks and the fish just lie around
like rank griddlecakes, but don't get discouraged,
we're taking care of all that. I tucked the note
back into my saddlebag and went out for the night,
hoping for a more attractive invitation
upon my return. But when I came back,
the saddlebag sat wide open on the desk
and a breeze blew through the drapes. I looked
at my old hands and blamed them. I left my shoes
in the kitchen. I stood at the center
of my enormous house, wondering why I stay.
I stay because muscadines grow on the trellis
out back and because of my two dogs.
We feast at daybreak. We brew our own shine.
No one comes to visit.

# Weakness #1: The Barber

He is cutting my hair. He is parting my red hair and smiling.
His hands are silver-beaked birds come north for the summer,
recovering daffodil bulbs, dove eggs, the pupas of monarchs
from my deepest reaches, holding each before me, then tucking it
inside his breast pocket. I am here to snap out of something,
to transform, and move on. Rain falls in blue ropes over the city,
the streets are turning with parasols. I've been told
this is the third stage of grief. After that, a yellow field.
He is twisting my hair in his hands, weaving a ladder in dream-state,
a bone-stark bridge of temptation; his eyes planets at dawn
when they look at me, planets at dusk when they look at me again.
I look like I've swallowed a rose and chase it down with a tumbler
of sparkling water. It's important to remember the room is actually here,
the white marble falling too close to the category: heaven.
Someone plays a cello in the alley. The notes enter the smoky hollow
of my mouth, and there is a silence. Eventually, loss will be nothing
more than a coat hung on the back wall. At dusk I will board
the slow boat home, buckling up for the shock of an emptied
    apartment,
the walls returned to their original bare, your dishes and books packed
and hauled across town. Starflowers explode in his mirror, swifts dive
in and out of the black chimneys. It's still raining, and good to be
    awake.

# Noiseless and Small

Homeless bees
are the saddest creatures
in the world and yet
so many violins inside me
and my little head.
I've got new buckles
and a waistcoat and
I'm hungry. My legs rub
together like she-crickets
in flames and blue tulips
sprout from the mattress.
An all-cymbal
marching band disperses
over the horizon.
Love turns cartwheels
in a drop of water.

# Wine

I chose the more rambunctious of the two
because it would be nice with the cockles,
which are smaller than clams with shorter necks
and larger stomachs. Bottled in '63,
it had a trace of tannin and tasted
like hickory smoke or an old book, leaves,
a leather boot, another person's tongue, rain,
chairs—mahogany chairs, the rings around a planet,
nudity, adult language,
stone, horse, loss,
pheasants and their beaks, feet,
a stamp from China, bloodstone,
a foreign country, no—a foreigner, an arched doorway.
And the soup: cream of beet with a dollop of cream.
Danish sea-fish decorated with spawn. A pot of chocolate
speared by a thin candle. An enormous wooden tub
of scalding water, half-moon, half-man,
framed by eaves and a phone line.
An iguana perched on the edge of the frigid air.
The whole world aged beyond reason.
The boy at the desk flashed the lights
to tell us our time was up. We had to hurry
because the pumice of grapes grew thin on our lips
and the ripe earth was turning in the leaves.

# Storm

Today I went to the river and promised to stay
until I was calm. A fisherman cast a net
into the slide of light and a boy offered me
three white rocks that he had found. As he walked away,
it occurred to me: he had not offered them at all,
he only wanted me to see. And I had said
*no thank you, sweetbun, keep them for yourself*
*little angel from the trees with one eye like a sparrow*
*and the other like a wren.* I frightened him
and everyone else on the path. I was alone,
so the couples out walking grew wary and the dogs
gone crazy with the joy found in water ran away
when I tried to touch them. This morning, I woke
in the arms of another and began to miss you
so hard my thighs ached. I thought I would break.
The horses across the river have been spooked
by a white bird and are running up a hill, toward
the darkening sky. The sound of hooves spreads
across the earth like heavy rain. There is nothing
like the feel of an enormous ribcage moving beneath you.
The mares cluster as the sire paces around in the wind.
I can hear him breathing.
He breathes like a man and I believe he too,
nurses a dark pit at the core of his being.
The fisherman has disappeared. A trout flits around

in the churning water like a nickel. I should
go home now. The trees are telling me it is night.

# Phone Call from China

three tornadoes demolished my hometown

your new city will be a river by august

your president was here yesterday
he changed his tie to match
my president's tie   they rode horses together
they are in love     and now  a killing spree

so you ate swan for the first time
selected your own from the carriage
the one with no eyes please

next  a crimson pangolin
with crushed hands   or crushed

what's on your feet? some kind of
wooden slipper   you sound hooved

yes  I know     but your voice

it is the loss of an arm
the arrival of a new tooth
a foot in the nook of its life's work

what are the flowers like? who is more beautiful?
the women or the flowers? don't answer that
no don't tell me   okay who?
your lips   a bee could get good

and blitzed off your lips   a bee could live
off the orchid in your eye for nine days
or more   in the study of light you call face

you have to go   and oh  a bus drifting
into a gorge nearly took your life

yes   I'm listening   yes   I hear you

locked in your room  you paint
a pine branch  meaning
to weave hair or bear melons
a woman lingering between
earth and sun  dreaming
a night in the rainforest  a star wrapped in a vine
august  fish confused by a chandelier

jacket suspended in a doorway
love   two fingers holding a tongue
two serpents embracing a thighbone
gravity attracting memory

each word  a monastery in the wind

and sounding like a thumbnail struck a tea bowl
an orange rolling downhill
thousands of children barking

and one child barking separately

# Miami in September

I am the heart of the burning chopper,
the burning muscle in the fist. Below me, a green ribbon of fish.

The heart, the flame, the firelock,

fie for shame. In my other life, I stroll the sea floor
masquerading as a man.

Let us try once to see another's hurting

and see instead the bodies of crickets, stacked and burning
in the name of children. Children, ha,

they smoke down the street throwing glass. I hear them laughing,
loud as hammers. I should claw out of here

because if I stay my head will drop off. And the men in the park,

the ones who screw there all night, won't hear it, won't come over,

and the trees will smell like spunk in the morning.
The rest of us will go walking,
trying to pretend nothing smells, and that we heard nothing

from our beds last night,
imagining what it's like to stay out,

licking strangers in the dark. This morning over your heads,

I burned, like a fist in a machine, a ribbon of fish below me.
In my other life,
I wear gold and watch girl-on-girl videos.

I love gold, I love it. I know the dangers of children,
and fear all things adult. My hair swims like little black fishes.

It's my other life, my man-life.
I do handstands and watch myself bob in the weird water,
my pink nose glowing.

In my other life, the trees don't stink,

and the stink doesn't drift through my window and sit at the edge
of my bed like a lonely parent. No. They smell like yellow-gold hair
   flashing

in early light, the strangeness of another's agitation,

other towns, other peoples,
a dead gator in the road, its teeth like babies' teeth. They smell like
girl-on-girl, another's hurting, the queer side of fucking,

something burning. They smell like fun.

# On the Day of Your Arrival

A waterdark mare stands in a field and remembers
nights spent charging through the desert:

the gilded saddles, the bridles woven with orchids,
the veiled men that rode her through fragile cities.

She sighs and thinks, *I cannot live on love alone.*

Gazeboes burn in the eyes of the mare.

Standing at the edge of the field for the first time,
she imagined gold tassels hanging from the sky and began

to weep, the field growing wide as the desert, dark as the blood
of horses. Stars crawled through the reeds like crickets.

# Inklings

After rain and the evening meal,
our nightsteps clicking,
my hand

curled birdishly in his,
we darken down the street,

a middle space of orange haze
strolling also.
Looking through

the window of a plant-filled house,
we imagine an existence of afterdinners:

a pine-green armchair, a finger
dipped in a cordial.

Slowly we travel,

two minds collecting noise
in a suburban corner of this silencita.
Half a mile down

the river bellycrawls through
its own dark banks. The last of the storm

comes down from the branches.

*

A glass of wine reflects onto his face,
illumined and shadowed,

as if looking into a pond at night.

A beetle blinks
in the garden like a lonesome smoker

at the wee-most hour,

in a twin darkness;
handlike plants pause against the rainy air.

*

I was reading on the porch,
and then asleep.
His bootsteps on the stairs

entered me,
they walked about inside.

When I woke he was beside me,

sleeping also.

*

My catacombs have surround-
sound, a gulf of iris
where quiet

begets quiet.
We take our meals

in a spooking stillness:

a flame twitching
like a goldfinch,

clink of silver

against the plates.
A low wind

takes the flame out.
Then a flora of dead-light

to which we are given.

*

A shell plugged into the wall
means we can see
the room. The sounds

of the body
are low darkling coos,

the rhythms of the breath
watching everything rise from the rafters

and disappear into the box of sky that turns
blue to rose to blood,

to clouded,

to starrish; dark little dovetunes

gone shrieklike,
birds taken from birds, the ones that flew

and the ones that did not.

# Somewhere Between Here and China

The heart is an apple.
The heart is a planet.
I wish I was an apple or a planet.
The heart is an eggplant.
The heart is a handful of grapes
wrapped in a fig leaf and placed
at the center of the table like a horn
filled with melon or a horned melon
next to a glass of kirsch.
The heart is stuffed with raisins.
The heart is needled with cloves.
The heart is cloven.
The heart is the butcher's glass case,
the butcher's mental block,
the butcher's red eye.
The heart closes when it wants to.
The snow is so pretty, the heart
can't leave it behind.
The heart cries out for the snow.
The heart would die for the snow.
The heart is a face. It carries
itself around in a basket. It plows
through wheat fields and blows
around in the grass and loves
the feel of wheat on its skin.
The heart drinks first from the watering hole.

The heart is a tongue. I wish I was a tongue
or a cloven foot or an eggplant.
The heart breaks plates.
The heart eats meat.
The heart weaves cloaks
for itself and its loved ones.
The heart chimes like forks
on a string in the wind. The heart is a spoon,
an empty glass with its wings
pinned to the wall. The heart gives thanks.
The heart crouches in the little shelters it has made.
The heart is a quiet gentleman tending its flocks
and wearing a pink bonnet in the sun.

It's snowing inside the heart.

The heart is a podling. The heart is a star cave.
The heart beckons and measures.
The heart grunts when poked and moans
with pleasure once every few days.
The heart whistles. The heart chirps.
The heart eats the meat of plants
and beats like the wand growing out
of the lily. The heart is a lily.
Wait, no it's not. The heart has never
been a flower. The heart is a hand.
The heart clings like a tiny bat.
The heart at pupa stage. The adult heart:
a case of old things, an intricate bracelet,
a box filled with newspaper clippings,

a little heart-shaped box all emptied out.
Whoever used to live here no longer
lives here. The possessions are divided
and marked for the children.
An antique quilt for the daughter,
gilded frames for the sons.
The heart is a brave cabbage.
The heart tastes just like cabbage.
It blooms like a flower and still
it is not a flower. The heart cleans itself.
The heart adjusts and adjusts.
The heart clicks its heels and brushes
its long dark hair. The heart turns into
a new heart every hour on the hour.
The heart is the size of a head.
It is filled with chambers and the chambers
are filled with fancy chairs.
The heart carries itself through life
and holds itself like a dying spider.
The heart is a wigwam of light, a lantern swinging
at the end of a pole. The heart lights the lake,
attracting minnows and the souls
of the drowned. The heart holds its breath
and wears a crown of daisies. The heart sighs.
The heart echoes inside.

Snow drifts into the mouth of the heart.

The heart dives into the ellipsis of the lanternlight.
The heart thinks the well is a mouth.

The well knows the heart to be wrong.
The heart throws its crown into the mouth
of the well and speaks to no one.
The heart is a flame. The heart. The heart.
I don't know what to do with this block of time,
this moment in space. It is unimportant
and impatient. It plumps like a gamebird
and takes off for the evening. The heart
is a young hen, a guinea in a pen.
The heart creeps around behind the curtains.
The heart makes homes for baby birds.
A brilliant sunset and the heart flies
for the first time ever. It sees the earth below
and gasps. It sees the coastline and feels
a little tinge of joy. It is always like this.

The heart sings as if caught on a branch.
The heart is a dark star, a bold and fast planet
careening through the universe.
I wish I was bold and fast and dark.
I wish I was a star cave or a gamebird,
with a crown of daisies and the shadow of a mouth.
I wish I was a spoon.

But I am a speck fading from the horizon,
always somewhere between here and China.
And the heart is a flower.

It's snowing inside the flower.

# Weakness #2: The Barber

Time for me to calm down,
for my fantasy life is rich but my hair grows
slow as the ancient tortoise.
Still, at night, it falls to the floor and he wraps
his strong body inside of it.
He holds his bones
against my bones and there is a flawless simplicity:
an arm through a sleeve,
a lantern inside a tree.
My hips open like a time-lapse rose,
parakeets bleat in my cochleae,
and I wake to find that loss has taken its leave of me.
I have waded across the yellow field
and know what I want now:
the ox-eye daisy in its carriage of twilight,
the afterimage in a doorway of someone
who wants to save me.

# Circles

The black stain of my body in the space left by branches
curves girlishly: the electric hair, the cinched waist.

Blessed am I.

I walk a street of day en absentia,
the Japanese strange trees domed over me.

Thank godliness.

Thank birdworlds.

Thank suspension of ire:
the crate swung over this beatitude,

the life pursued mainly at night. The path to the creek
is lit with white rocks and a hole blows at path's end.

The den lamp killed in the brown house,
streetbulbs cease their ringing and spread to darker corners of the grass.

Evening's thrombosis: the silence that follows me,

soft foot thuds giving speed to the red vessel of my breast.
The things I seek then don't want anymore creep around

like the day's failures, making holes in a night that worries me.
I walk toward the sound of water over pebbles,

toward what I want:
a few undeathly connections,

love without occlusion, open as an ear and truthful,
tonguelessly so.
Leopard rain falls in the hollow where we

take each other weeknights. Soft voices repeat themselves
in the yellow leaves. And there, the afterhours call

of branch lizards who freeze when I pass
embalmed in the fleck-sized concerns of a softened life.

The moment squats grapishly.

I walk about inside it, fairly even and satisfied at summer's close.
I should offer alms to the long neck of water,

that which stretches between supper and first light and returns,

undaunted. The circle of arms awaiting me in the front hall.
The burning lanterns. The rooms leading into other rooms.

# Late Afternoon July

A rose-covered casket with music inside
makes its way down my street. Or maybe
a huge music box with a body inside.
The day passes like a boy running through
the woods. I mistake every tree for a man.
I wander off the path and appear in someone else's
backyard, staring into their living room.
A sliver of lemon waves from the bottom
of my glass and shouts "pay attention to me!"
But I can't. I lift my hand and a gleaming river
makes its way to my brain, so life seems a little better
than it did fifteen minutes ago. A light breeze
and I think briefly of palm trees at dawn,
a bicycle rickshaw under a streetlamp, the idea
of future, meaning chairs in the garden, arbor
of blue grapes, an enormous rose-covered
birthday cake at least twice a year. I can't feel my feet.
A car with no muffler and one arm extended
from the passenger window trolls past. The air
is filled with creatures that become more beautiful when still.
Now someone's tapping the side of a mug or drainpipe.
It's raining. A crane is swallowing a frog.
The living room is poppy red. The house
is filled with people who love each other more
than the flowers. And as I turn to walk home

in the tropical light, the house stands behind me
like a quarry. A star hangs over that quarry.

# A Night in the Village

My mother said *burn these letters when I'm gone.*
She said *when you marry, put this handkerchief in your shoe,*
*don't look at it till then,* and she clamped the box shut.

Like everyone else a century ago, she was the color of sepia.
A child, he said *take this off,* and I climbed
on top of him. Where was she that night?

In her boudoir dusting her neck with violet powder
or in the shed heaving an axe into her still-lifes?
I pressed my ear to his chest and it held on

like a shell. My mother said *I'm going to meet my lover,*
*the one on the horse.* My sisters opened her closet
and rolled around in her furs. She said *Alys,*

*you get the opal. Isabel, the pearls are for you.*
*Della, take the watch.* She said *throw me in the ocean.*
She said *those rooks in the freezer, throw them out,*

*they belonged to your father.* And on the brightest day
of the year, we let her go a teaspoon at a time.
My brother comes to me every night now.

His little hands web like pipistrelles in my hair
and his small throat trills like a reed pipe. Across the hall,
my sisters warm their brandy over candles. They say

*we hear you.* They say *you just won't listen, will you.*
Listen. The rooks are burning branches in the yard.

# Even Donkeys

I honor the light and the dark inside you.
What do you honor?

*How much would you give me to eat this?*

I once spent ten days in a purified silence. It was hard,
and I learned to like people better. What did you ever learn?

*How much for whatever's in this bowl?*
*I'd say it's been in here a good six months.*

Do you know what a dipterist studies?

*C'mon, how much?*

Not a penny. Do you like my friends?

*No.*

Okay then. How about my family?

*Not especially.*

My co-workers? My grocer? That lady that always asks me for a dollar?

*No. No. No. Ooh, look at this. A rotten grape. How much?*

What kind of person do you want to be?

*A rich one.*

I want to be kind and gentle. I want to raise butterflies.

*I want to be rich and more rich. I want to make money and spend it.*

I can't plant tomatoes though. That I simply won't do.

*You won't need to. We got farmstands.*
*Here we go, blue-cloudy barbecue sauce. To drink the whole bottle.*
*Name your price, lover, name your price.*

Seventy-five cents. No water chasers.

*Or okay, how about this stuff here? It's really old. Maybe some kind of pasta.*
*Maybe a bean salad from the party.*

When you dream, what do you dream about?

*Money.*

Is that all? Because I dream about going to prison for crimes I didn't
    commit.
I dream about sex with donkeys and being forced into stuff. I dream
    about rooms
leading into other rooms. You ever dream about donkeys?

*I dream about being rich.*

I dream about blue-faced people, drown victims exhumed from
the Atlantic, found just offshore in propeller planes, still buckled in
   but their hair
flying around like French medusas.

*You dream about rich people.*

Death dressed in Prada.
Death walking the sea floor in a Prada suit.

*Right, exactly. That's how he dresses. I wanna go out just like that.*

Imagine the vessel settled onto the sand.
And death strolling over in this suit, he's handsome,

bending to peer into the watery chamber,
checking his watch, giving a little wave.

*Beautiful. How much for these little corn thingies if I dip them in the
   sauce?*

They look as if they don't believe.

*This milk skin.*

They look predetermined, as if designed to die that way.

*This orange rind with a wart on it.*

And nothing about it is funny. Imagine a world in which nothing is
   funny.
Imagine an obese clown going out through the window, big red feet last.

*This mothy larval crud.*

Imagine the sky left when he is gone.

*How much?*

How much for what?

*How much for the clown?*

I don't know, like a million dollars probably.
Why, what are you gonna do?

*Ha.*

Ha ha.

*Ha ha ha.*

No really, what are you gonna do?

# Crowcrowscrows

Night landed like crows on the lemon field.

By morning "the rinds had formed a vast marigold"—
as recorded by the black box of an airplane.

Each crow flew off with a lemon in its belly,
*peaches grow south of Worcester*
like Möbius strip in each crow brain.

Such wonders in store for tomorrow's passengers
who will be told to peer out their windows,
"witness a field of flesh."

*

The bikers rode over the hill like crows
with lights on their chests. They'd spent half the day

writing stories on vellum, and needed to calm

their nerves. So a drive through Sunderland
where they pass us with our top down,

our hair blazing through the afternoon,

he still sucking his meal through a straw.
They say if he weren't French, he'd be fine by now.


&ast;


All the black boxes have been painted orange
so we can find them in the water.

Little cabbage,
what if we were to paint every crow bright orange?

*We would kill them to make hats*
*much like we killed the quetzal and now*

*his virgin coinage is nowhere to be found.*
*The howler monkeys know,*
*but they're not talking.*


&ast;


Marigolds are the flowers of grief.
French astronauts tuck them in their socks before missions

to remember what they lose
when they leave this planet, and why they should come back.


&ast;

My parents are turning in the soil,
which disturbs the crows and means it's time for me to hush.
It's time for you to hush too, petit bisson.


*


Teenagers conjure spirits by the river.
They say if you call long enough

the river will slide into a figure eight
and light will play along its inner walls,
formulaic shadows of who you are and how much longer

you're going to be here. We stay away.
It's where the crows eat mangosteen.

The leather bells drop to the mud and crack:
crescents of white meat along the banks
like eyes at various stages of open and closed.

Mangosteen: queen of fruits.

We stay away from there.
We drive all night when we have to.

# The Iris of the Pig

Beside the head, the meats swing.

The flattened canvas of his body hangs

in a door of sunlight.
His pigcap, his yellow hair, his teeth

extracted and floating in the display bowl:
how they clack when we're not looking.

See how your hand looks behind the screen
they made of him,                                    .
as if your hand could live alone inside him,

his flesh rolled and pressed to silk, the thinned-out papers
of his blood, the scarlet cloud of him.

Your hand

open.
Closed.

Open,
the iris of the pig, eyeball of the dead.

Three years of digging and at last, found:

two dog cemeteries, one 2" calf figurine, four fucklamps,
and one banana[1]
(female, late 20's, blunt instrument).


Their majesty wrote *my city before my children*
then burned the city himself and moved his family eastward.
So they lived.


Or they did not live.
Their bathhouses, their cruel eating habits: what?


Little door, yon eyelet:


probably beneath the pink lid, a tube of black chickadees,
rain in shades of a bride driving a car.
From here,


I can see her make-up, the fragrant oilslick of her hairdo.


Beneath his skull plate and his brain's fatted folds,


we may well find a vast and buried city, the baby's dust
in an olive jar stored near what may have been
a bedroom. True:


a pig screams when held. And sometimes the posthumous eye
stares out, wildly frigid.

---

1 In the city of Ashkelon, an excavated human is called a "banana."

But sometimes it lies still and flat,
a low slope of flesh with a world inside,
if a foggy world, if knuckle-size, if only the one after this.

Here I come, in my pigcoat,
facing the wrong direction. Here I come

with the icepick, the toothbrush, a legend for the language.
Who shall I find today?
And what number shall I give him?

Open: the eyeball of the pig,

blinking once for yes, and once more for yes.
See the cheeks dissolved by the metal in the facepaint.
See the dogs wearing crowns to their death.

See how your hand is not your hand.

And the city itself,
how it glistens.

# La Reforma

Night: ink spilling across a newspaper.

Morning: ink rolling back the other way,
darkness making room for a photograph in which I sit

at a tiny table, staring into a bowl.
In the supermarket, I bought a sack of black mushrooms.
They looked conscious

and went well with the calamari. The day pauses,
and forks itself:

quilts of yellow dust, a veil of rain, trees. The purl of their leaves.

Once I mistook burning leaves for rising birds
and once for callous impulses,

but that was epochs ago.

Look at me, with a dress in my arms,

staring into the frozen window and beyond you,
strange pietà behind a glass wall

then flash after flash, a surface of blind spots.
How we melt and collide inside
until what's left is a throng of people holding cameras.

The painting of a lazy bride surrounded by maids
was once a dead girl being readied for the grave. It hung, and hangs,

in the corridor:
*look closely so you can see where the artist painted the eyes open*
*to make a gift for his granddaughter.* And again his voice,

this time through the keyhole:

*when you were but a truffle I wrapped us in a giant leaf*
*and held on till we bathed in green light*

Then the tip of his finger, also through the keyhole. Waving to me.

His eye in the keyhole. Blinking.
As a young man, he was attractive. Dark and pale and dark.

But please never tell him I said so.

After a night's rain, the soil is dotted with mushrooms,
those said to erase memory. Like the hydra that grow on internal organs,

how they swell with light and bend as if to weep.
Listen: a ting off a tooth,
the tongue sliding across the slick bar of teeth.

Ting. White bricks. Ting.

*** 

In a cube of dotted light,

I watch a woman named Pam accept a throat tube,
a doctor's gloved hand near Pam's shoulder,
Pam sliding into a white drawer.

Pam the iota.

Pam on mute.

Pam the speck in the rug at which I stare,
and well into the night. Once I mistook dust for a swarm of bees

(they came rising from the ground)

and their hymns for horns, resounding through my daze.
But they were dust, and collapsed

into the flowers grown black against the iron sky,
the way the smile darkens to a rind
and the snow behind us turns to soil. The world sucked

through a lens and returned, this time with the left arm sprouting
from the wrong side of the body,

the body slick with tears and held in the arms like a robe
from the wash.

The bowl on the table glimmered with tendrils,
pink and blue tubes,
barnacles in broth.

Listen: the horns on t.v.,
the bees diving back into the earth.

He's sliding notes under the door now:
*remember those wind-flowers  how we clipped the head from one*
*and two more grew in its place*

*how the sun entered the marrow*
*and the bones*
*shone*

Someone circles the thing blooming near my shoulder.
The bulb, like a battery in the blood,

flickers and stings, pisses, and saunters away,
this time quietly through the night, then up into the burnt-out tree
   hole,

where it builds a bed of twig and sings of itself till morning.

# Three Days Before

Three days before you die, your head gets smaller.
The skin of your neck loosens.

He stood in my kitchen, telling me about the chest his mother sent
    from Germany,
his teeth big as rocks. Then he went upstairs to settle in with a book

and a plate of sausage. Three days before you die, the skin of your
    neck loosens.
He said he was born with teeth.

The door behind him stood open, and I thought of the eggs in the
    icebox.
Silhouettes of baby chickens in blue ovals.
Like loony toon eggs when the farmer holds up a match,

and the unborn gives a little wave. He stood in my kitchen,
and looked like someone was sneaking up behind him with a pail of
    cold water.

I was trying not to laugh and spoil the joke.

He stood there, smiling at me, telling me all about the chest his
    mother sent
from Germany. I kept thinking *when were you born? When did you
come here?*

And the whole time the guy with the water getting closer
and me trying not to laugh and also thinking, *when were you born?
and why did she mail that chest?*

*It must weigh two hundred pounds.*

Between three and four this morning, your heavy leg slid from mine.

A star erased itself through a slit in the blinds. Your eyelid quaked as if
something had just come at you, bigger than it should be,
wearing a suit of feathers and flapping its arms. As the thing disappeared

and you turned away, I pressed my hand to your back to say *you will
    not blow
through this world.* A bird sung once then stopped, too dark.

The checker told me it's best to drink tea. Tea preserves the body
so that two hundred years from now, they can open our boxes and make

decisions as to how to live their own lives.
When they open my box, they will find a teaspoon of ash and a card
    that reads:
Mother Always Loved You.

The bagger's moustache hangs on either side of his mouth,
little brown legs that startle me when he smiles. Three days before
    you die,

your chest moves inward. A dent grows between your pectoral muscles.
Some people are born like this.
He wore a t-shirt, but I could see through the fabric

and he seemed smaller, caved in. The t-shirt just sort of hanging
    around him.
He looked like a child. And when the t-shirt lifted slightly,

and dropped slightly, like a white butterfly. Now the guy behind him
    had a net.

And he still didn't notice. And we were trying not to laugh and give
the whole thing away. It was going to be so funny,

when he was standing there with a net on his head,
smiling at me with those big white rocks, his eyes bulging like ovum,
dark baby chickens in his pupils,

his head getting smaller.

Then he would start laughing too,
but he wouldn't think it nearly as funny as we did. I kept thinking

*when did you come here? Who did you come with?*
And he was standing there, smiling at me with teeth like white stones,
the kind in the garden path, stones that show up at night.

See the girl, lit by white stones.

Her pale blue face. Membrane of milk over bird bones.
Between three and four this morning,

a bird sang once, then stopped, too dark. What kind of bird?
You didn't hear it.

Moist with sweat, you turned away from the wild-armed thing
in your dream. I was holding you down, so you wouldn't drift out
the window and over the town and away.

For a while, I could hear him snoring.
A soft children's program kind of snore. A fuzzy trill.

A feather rising and falling over the lips.
He slept.

And then he did not sleep.
On the mattress we drove to the dump a few days later.
I kept thinking *who are these people? Where are their children?*

He stood in my kitchen.
He did not lean. He stood upright with his hands at his sides.
There's a ham in the icebox, I kept thinking.

Maybe if I give it to him, he will go away. He was talking about
the chest his mother sent from Germany. And I was thinking
*why Germany? Which kind of person are you?*

*Why did you come here?* The ham in my icebox sat alone in the dark.

Pink meat on an elbow bone.
And a fish on a plate. Inside the open mouth,
a purple-black tongue

like the tip of a broken toe.
Three days before you die, your arms get thinner,
and hang from your torso as if attached by thread.

He stood in my kitchen and the lights were humming.
Long tubes of flies.
Three days before you die,

your back rises and your shoulders hunch.
Your chin drops.
He stood in my kitchen. He said he'd seen his father for the last time

when he was twelve, moving backward in a boat destined for here.
I kept thinking about a naked man strung up in a tree,

the bird's nest at his groin, the autonomous thumb.
The river snaking beneath him as he turned silently on the rope,
head down, beneath a rag of black hair.

Creak of the branch.
Little growths along the bough, like a row of pink buttons.

He stood in my kitchen, his teeth big as rocks.
I would have thought his ears would remain large as well,
like elaborate chanterelles spreading out from the sides of his
    diminishing head,

soft and a little rubbery, with brown spots on the edges.
But his ears also grew smaller.

More like truffles sliced paper-thin with a razor.
Translucent wafers half-hidden by the damp tufts of his hair,

his bird ears.

Once I ordered a truffle from a French catalogue.
It arrived in a shining black box with Japanese characters on the top
and *ne touche pas a mon pote* on the bottom.

Auriculars: the formal name for bird ears.

A young bird can learn the songs of other birds,
so the birds over our heads are often multilingual.

What bird sang outside our window this morning?
And did it sing in its own language, or was it trying to fool us?

A cardinal with the tongue of a wren, a jay with the beak of a finch.
Who knows? We don't. We pay little attention to the life outside this
    room.

Now that I think about it, he looked nearly gone.

He stood in my kitchen, looking nearly gone. I was thinking about
the icebox, what I could give him to take upstairs,
what needed to be thrown out.

How it all sits there in the dark: empty mayonnaise jar,
lavender bruise on a kiwi, the eggs.
The bone, that fish.
Starry body of the fish, gleaming in the icebox as it did

at the bottom of the lake.
Between three and four this morning, what kind of bird cried out
as your heavy leg slid from mine and I kissed

your warm back and fell asleep again? Why did it cry out?
What did it see in its diurnal fleck of brain? Three days before you die,

what do you forget about the world outside your room?
And what do you remember?
Where did he come from? And what caused his descending aorta

to send a ball of grief to his ascending aorta so early this morning,
after a day in the woods, after dinner, and a concert?

The widow descends and ascends the stairs all day,

carrying garbage bags. She offered you a suit, gray wool/good
   condition.
I told her no, that you don't need any new things right now.

Can you imagine? walking around in his old suit?
You could hardly get one leg in.

His chicken suit.

When my chest feels held by an iron hand,

when I can't sleep, I think of a leather shoe falling slowly to the bottom
of a lake, and the foot inside. The shoe come to rest
on the silt floor. The foot's flesh like the chewed flesh of a morel

growing in a warm broth, flowering saprophyte,
a hand falling open from a deep sleep,

how it feels to eat flesh, if only the flesh of a truffle. A horned truffle.
Press your ear to it, you might hear the rushing sounds of water.
You might hear a song. A voice from the other side of this world.

A distant tongue.
How it rattles and quips. How it quivers and squeaks.

A *lalala* that could go on forever.
He stood in my kitchen, with his ear turning pink, like a communion
    wafer on a tongue.
The white circle fading.

His bird ears fading. Only the auriculars remaining.
Three days before you die,

your pants seem to stand on their own.
Your legs float around like wires inside. We don't notice
until you're gone. We might say *have you lost weight?*

but never *tonight you learn the tongue of a distant bird.*
We only realize it later, when we remember

how you looked standing there, the guy with the net standing behind
     you
and grinning. So hard not to laugh,
with your eyes bulging, darkened chicks in your pupils, your head
     getting smaller.

Nearly gone.

He stood in my kitchen, smiling at me with his mouth of stones.
See the girl on the garden path.
The soft bluelight around her ankles, like the light from a vein.

The last time he saw his father, he was twelve,
moving backward in a boat destined for here. His father's voice like a
     broom

against the cold air,
his stained hands hanging from his coat sleeves. Goodbye in Romanian:
quick stab of the broom at a moth on the wall. How it sounded

to a boy in a boat, drifting backward one clear morning.

I was thinking about the freezer, that I should defrost it. His head had
     become smaller.
And I didn't notice. I didn't notice the guy with the net, or the one
     with the pail,

until now.

And now I know.
Three days before you die, your head becomes smaller.

Your neck falls in delicate flaps. Your chest fades to negative beneath
the soft fabric of your clothes. I can almost see it,

barely moving in and out. The shadow of a thorax.
Bombyx mori:
the name of a moth that can no longer fly, that requires human care
    to survive.

It breathes and feeds in a lab in Monterey,
in a simulated trunk of winter clothes. The belly a lime-colored lump.
The wings, opalescent flakes.

Tiny dent of a frown in the top of its head.
Between three and four this morning, our skin glowed. Between three
    and four

this morning, a bird sang once. Your leg slid from mine.
Then stopped. I pressed my hand against your back. Too dark.
You will not blow through this world.

My love, you will not blow through this world. See how our skin glows.
Lampskin.

Listen, to what we should have heard this morning between three and
    four:
a girl looking in the window,

a bird,

a leg.

A boat pulling away from a pier. Too dark.

How do I say the word without the trembling chin?

How do I make a broom of my voice?

What did we look like, lying there in the glowing tangle of limbs?

Like lamps.

Listen, the sound of grief leaving the body.

See the girl talk to the young boy.

See her lead him to the river, taking his hand in her bird-bone hand.

See his face when they return, as if he'd seen,

what?

Water moving backward.

You, my love, you will not blow through this world.

You walk this place in marble shoes. You with your lion coat,

you with your club. Three days before you die, your head gets smaller.

Your skin becomes fragile as a delicacy.

How you glow in the wee hours. Like a postwar lamp.

How you glow.

Words don't last, they grow apart. Like the meat of a fruit, how it
    pulls apart.
The cotton meat of turned fruit.

From rose-tinged to bitter to fluid.
How the mouth darkens. The pickled wall of flesh, the swollen tongue,
the indigo bulb of tongue.

The legacy of smallness, of feeling like a dot in the dirt.

He stood in my kitchen, like an insect trapped in a tube.
A humming sound and the noise of birds. The eggs, buzzing in the
    icebox.

The foot reaching the surface of the lake. The shoe tossing on the
    silvery bottom.
What excess sleep will do to the body. When escorted down the path,
you may be asked to sing or count.

You may be told to give thanks, or step more quickly.

Keep singing. *Lalala.*
Dirge, sonata, hell-bound baritone.

Till no one hears you.

He was born with teeth. He was nearly gone when I got there.
How she will miss him. How I will miss you someday, *mon pote.*

The girl in the garden walks through the late October veil,

the distance between summer and winter.
There's a star in the aperture,
and a cold wind coming through.

See the white circles. They're fading.

Only the water, at rest now, remaining.

# The Primitive Model

At rage o'clock we painted up,

vinyl, gold, liquid red;
lawless and going to get lawless, busting out the cups with cash,

and rode from the smoking city with the top down.
Strobes of moonshine across the boneblack clouds.

They say Russians found him. But where did they carry him off to?
We kept one eye to the ground, and one to the starry morning on its
    way.


\*


Afghanistan is now the capital of the world
and flights have never been cheaper.

We drive faster than hell down a thin black highway.

He landed in Kazakhstan and slept in the sand
three days before found.
The craft burned to a flake but he lives to tell,

soon as he wakes.

This much we know:
no one shall darken the door of that space station again.


\*


In the museum: exhibit lingua flagellate.
A pride of green ladies with lips tacked to their noses.

Earlessness. The pink years. I studied and studied
and still don't know what the artist wanted to say.


\*


And now, I wear the red tarboosh,
my fingers singed and barely hanging on.

And he asleep in the back seat, like a boy with a glass head.


\*


Rings of fire glisten through the cracks in a tobacco barn.
The sky is a time-lapse rose

and backlights the claws of plants. How one world resembles another,
which is what W said three minutes before she died.

Do you see it? The slit in the air
and the two legs dangling.

Fog roams the valley,
swallowing elk to their necks and sweeping them along,
the way trees once looked at the edge of a field in winter.

# Shelburne Falls

A hand in a crevice, the tongue at rest in the mouth,
and also,
the pressure of one body against another: summer, waxed and
    honeyed.

Rain on the motorbike, rain on the helmet.
Worms on hooks drift beneath the river's surface.

   \*\*\*

On the bridge of flowers,
a bushel of sweet pea, half-open yellow pods; the tropicanas bleed and
    fade.

Say it, you were alone. You were alone.

On Nightbeat,
a woman's face split like a potato by a bullet, her eye on a spring,
she'd meant to lodge it in her brain, of course.

That's you on the bridge of flowers, watching a dime drop into the
    water.
That's you in the restaurant, nursing a clam plate.

Say it, this life we share, it will not do.

76

This dusty house.
These lackluster friends.
These children, and all their friends.

   ***

Here comes my brother, in his woe suit,
                     his woe shoes,
                           his woe hat.

Last time we saw him he waved from a ledge of blue light,
his belongings in a paper sack:

*goodbye, goodbye.*
Now he's here again, in his woe car,
                 with his woe dog,
                      how he yowls outside the door.

And all my cousins, in a local motel, watching strippers

play with fruit;
the room with pictures of horses on the walls, the ones with white
   blazes.

   ***

From here, I watch young boys leap from the rocks.

And there you are, hurling yourself into the air and mooning us.
And then the girl,

who chickened and slipped.
Her ear leaked as they pulled her pale body from the water.

Say it, you were alone. *I was alone.*

And the girl fell from the rocks,
and then what? *Her head struck,*
*her ear leaked. I was painting my toes and imagining the deaths*

*of loved ones. She interrupted me.*

Whether the bullet rents the face or buries itself in the skull,
if it blows through the heart,

still, the world, it grows less and less familiar.

    \*\*\*

One town over, a man sketches before dawn,
wingéd humans, only he's serious. His wife carves an ear out of clay.

Two towns over, a one-legged teen poses naked for a magazine.

Listen, seeds shaking in a paper ball,
the banana vendor's whistling.

    \*\*\*

Someday I'll hear it,
the footsteps of my children as they stop to watch the video,

me when I lived with my brand-new cat eyes:

*she was plump and fell with a noise*
*blood leaked from her ear and a large man pulled her from the water*


   ***

Summer: a body rebuilt. Then another.

We arrived in sunlight and drove off in sunlight,

sunlight through rain. Summer: nude and barely breathing,
the sky turning pink and a hush in the willow tops,

love by the humming light,
                    field stars.

That's you knee-deep in river water, thin as a crane.
That's you working the lure from a fish throat.

We're snaking back around now.

We're cheering as the bull enters the woman,
as half-light falls on the roses.
This world

peculiar and at the same time, filled with horses,
large photographs of horses,

their heads on fire.

# Long Goodbye

See the body. It is small and thin.
How the bones show through the skin.
See the flecks of polish on the nails,
the nail polish called glitter moth.
Touch the head. Listen for chimes.
Allow your hand through the hair,
the pale hair spread in the mad science light
of mid-morning rain. Press your lips to the feet.
The glitter from the party stuck to the toes
sticks to your lips. Your lips glimmer
like moths by the orange bulb, like rain
on a queue of white shoes in the grass,
like a starry two a.m. and the hole made
by a wild night, through which boys
in white nightshirts step calmly, and descend.
See the body. Still beneath the sheet.
The rain in the window falling sideways
like moths moving westward.
In the room with high ceilings,
in the room with one lamp on,
in the room where you first touched me, see the body.
In the room where paintings lean against the walls.
In the room where you stroke your bare chest,
where you comb and comb your gold hair.
In the room, in the room, in the room where we first
made it, where you pressed your lips to it,

wrapped your big fingers round it,

slid your bold hand right through it. See the body.

Small and thin. Tired and worn. The head bells,

the circles, the room without windows. The room

with the radio on; talk of visitation, talk of fata morgana,

installments of light, boxes of air and darkness,

in the room with no light in it. In the room where we first touched it.

In the room where we were born, where we will die.

See the body. The rageless body. Tell me, what do *you* do with yours?

In the room with one lamp on, what do *you* do, and how?

You have seen it, you have touched it, so was it good?

And did you feel the need to cry when it was done?

There there, they are bringing it out now.

They carry it through the tin corridor of voices

and through the back door. Wrapped in gossamer,

wrapped in cerecloth, in wire, in rosevine,

in silk thread from the shoe factory, in webbing, in chains,

in rope. See the body, wrapped in thread from the shoe factory.

Thread made of stolen horses. Thread made of dogs.

Threads of rain.

The body wrapped and left in the driveway.

The body rolling into the street.

Polish on the nails peeking out of the shroud, glitter on the feet.

Wave farewell to the body. Sing to the body as it rolls down the hill,

into the grove and toward the river. Throw marigolds and sing.

Throw doveblooms and sing. Throw a white rose and sing.

Sing low, sing high, sing never come back here again.

# THE AUTHOR

**Carrie St. George Comer** received her MFA from the University of Massachusetts, where she was awarded the Academy of American Poets prize. Her poems have appeared in *APR, Fence, New Orleans Review, Web Conjunctions, The Iowa Review,* and she was the recipient of the 2001 *Black Warrior Review* Prize in Poetry. She lives in Miami Beach and teaches at the University of Miami.

Benjamin Alsup

# THE KATHRYN A. MORTON PRIZE IN POETRY

1995 *The Lord & the General Din of the World*
by Jane Mead
Selected by Philip Levine

1996 *When*
by Baron Wormser
Selected by Alice Fulton

1997 *The Gatehouse Heaven*
by James Kimbrell
Selected by Charles Wright

1998 *Garden of Exile*
by Aleida Rodríguez
Selected by Marilyn Hacker

1999 *Summons*
by Deborah Tall
Selected by Charles Simic

2000 *World's Tallest Disaster*
by Cate Marvin
Selected by Robert Pinsky

2001 *The Darker Fall*
by Rick Barot
Selected by Stanley Plumly